The postman calls at a thatched cottage on this 1905 postcard, one of a long series of photographic cards published by the Photochrom Company.

PICTURE POSTCARDS

C. W. Hill

The Shire Book

Published in 2007 by Shire Publications Ltd,
Cromwell House, Church Street, Princes Risborough,
Buckinghamshire HP27 9AA, UK
(Website: www.shirebooks.co.uk)

British Library Cataloguing in Publication Data:
Hill, C. W. (Cuthbert William)
Picture postcards. – 2nd ed. – (The Shire book)
1. Postcards – History
I. Title 741.6'83
ISBN 0 7478 0398 6

Printed in Great Britain by Ashford Colour Press,
Unit 600, Fareham Reach, Fareham Road, Gosport,
Hampshire PO13 0FW.

Cover: *A selection of picture postcards from the author's collection.*

Some of the London flower-girls immortalised by George Bernard Shaw in his play 'Pygmalion', which opened at His Majesty's Theatre, London, in April 1914.

Contents

ERNEST E. WHITE,　　　　　STOURBRIDGE.

Miss Martha Green poses at a makeshift stile with a painted backcloth in Ernest White's studio in Stourbridge, about 1870, for a carte-de-visite photograph.

Introduction

As a young married woman in the 1890s the author's grandmother would see her husband off to his town office each morning, glance at the daily newspapers and then take her dog for a short walk. Into the pillar box at the end of the road she would drop a postcard to her butcher, telling him the cuts of meat she needed for dinner that evening. Within an hour or so the postman would empty the pillar box, and the postcard would be sorted and delivered by the midday post. Early in the afternoon the butcher's boy would bring the meat, in good time for the cook to prepare it for the evening meal.

Sold to raise funds for the Royal National Lifeboat Institution, this postcard reproduces a painting by Bernard F. Gribble (1873-1962). (Raphael Tuck & Sons)

The speed and convenience of this arrangement depended on two factors: the number of daily postal deliveries in Britain, at least four in most provincial towns and as many as seven in London, and that comparatively new feature of the postal services, the plain postcard, first introduced as an experiment in October 1869 in the Austro-Hungarian empire. The experiment proved so successful, with sales of the new cards estimated at a million every month, that other countries quickly adopted the scheme. The first British postcards were placed on

Above left: *A pleasing portrait of Santa Claus on an American postcard posted in New York on 23rd December 1910. (H. Wessler)*

Above right: *Before the First World War many postcards for the British and American markets were printed in Germany. This example, 'To my Valentine', was posted in Leacock, Pennsylvania, on 11th February 1909.*

sale on 1st October 1870. Made of pale buff card, they measured $3^1/2$ by $4^3/4$ inches (89 by 122 mm). On one side, printed in purple, they had the inscription 'POSTCARD – THE ADDRESS ONLY TO BE WRITTEN ON THIS SIDE', the royal coat of arms and a halfpenny stamp with an unflattering profile portrait of Queen Victoria. The other side of the postcard was left blank for the message.

Companies and tradespeople immediately recognised the commercial benefits of being able to advertise their wares and services at half the current letter rate of postage. Other citizens were at first less enthusiastic, fearing that their correspondence might be read by the postman or the servants and that fastidious friends might be offended at receiving a halfpenny postcard instead of a penny letter. These scruples were soon overcome, especially when postcards bearing pleasantly lithographed views of mountains, lakes, cities and spas began arriving from friends on holiday in such countries as Austria, Italy, Switzerland and Germany. In Britain the development of the holiday postcard was hindered by the insistence of the Post Office that

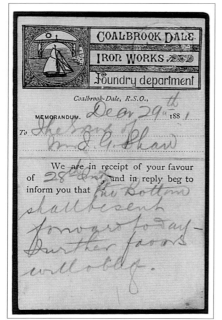

Above: *An example of the first British plain postcards, posted in Wigan on 22nd October 1871 to John Shaw & Son, Merchants, Wolverhampton.*

Left: *The Coalbrook Dale Iron Works used plain postcards with a pictorial heading showing the famous Iron Bridge and a Severn trow. This example, dated 19th December 1881, informed the Executors of Mr J. G. Shaw that 'We are in receipt of your favour of 28th inst. and in reply beg to inform you that the Bottom shall be sent forward today – Further favors will oblige!'.*

only the officially printed postcards would be accepted at the half-penny rate of postage. Privately printed postcards were liable to the full letter rate of postage, one penny. Another hindrance was the regulation, in other countries as well as Britain, that one side of the postcard must be reserved for the postage stamp and the addressee's name and address. Any picture had to share the other side of the postcard with the message. The British Post Office discontinued the postage penalty on privately printed postcards in 1894 and from 1902 allowed the address and the message to be written on the same side of the postcard, that bearing the postage stamp. The latter concession opened the way for enterprising publishers to market postcards depicting every scene and subject imaginable. German printers were already geared to produce picture postcards of high quality at low prices, so that many Edwardian views of British holiday resorts, beauty spots and historic buildings are inscribed as having been printed in Saxony or Bavaria.

Origins

Although the introduction of plain postcards can be precisely dated at 1869, various kinds of printed ephemera that preceded them clearly influenced their development into picture postcards. In May 1840, as part of Rowland Hill's scheme of uniform cheap postage, post offices in Britain began selling not only the first adhesive postage stamps, the celebrated Penny Blacks and Twopenny Blues, but also pictorial envelopes and wrappers.

Designed by an Irish artist, William Mulready RA, they depicted Britannia seated on a rock with a lion at her feet and despatching messengers with letters to the corners of the earth symbolised by assorted figures of Indians, Arabs, native Americans and Chinese. The allegory proved too trite even for the early Victorians, and to Rowland Hill's surprise the public acclaimed the neat and convenient little postage stamps while deriding the 'Mulreadies', as they were dubbed.

Despite their unpopularity the Mulreadies prompted the production of other kinds of pictorial envelope. Some were comic skits on the Mulready design, but many were intended to publicise social and political campaigns, among them those against slavery in the United States, intemperance in Britain and, less worthily, compulsory vaccination to prevent smallpox. Other designs supported an Anglo-American campaign launched during the 1840s for cheaper postage between Britain

Above: *In 1840, as part of Sir Rowland Hill's scheme of uniform cheap postage, the British Post Office issued envelopes and wrappers in this allegorical design by William Mulready, RA.*

Right: *The golden jubilee of Sir Rowland Hill's scheme of uniform penny postage was marked in 1890 by an exhibition at Guildhall, London, and the issue of commemorative postcards.*

Above: *Victorian illustrated notepaper usually featured conventional landscapes, but this example, posted from HMS 'Royal Albert' on 25th April 1856, showed 'The United Service landing in the Crimea'.*

Right: *A Christmas card of the 1880s in carte-de-visite size but lithographed in colour and meant to be posted in an envelope.*

Below left: *The Duke of Kent (1902-42) on a postcard in a series given with tins of De Reszke cigarettes in 1935 to mark the Silver Jubilee of the Duke's father, King George V.*

Below right: *Her short hair and her turban place this French girl in the 1920s. (Roto)*

Left: *Studio-posed sentimental photographs masked the grim realities of the First World War. This French example is captioned 'Under gunfire for France, accept this word of hope'. (Katz)*

Above: *The Italian artist Angelo Asti (1847-1903) produced portrait postcards for several publishers. This example, entitled 'Juliet', is from Raphael Tuck's 'Connoisseur' series.*

and the United States. Like the Mulreadies, these propaganda envelopes were designed so that their slogans and illustrations occupied the upper part and the edges at either side of the front, leaving the lower part clear for the addressee's name and address, an arrangement similar to that of the first picture postcards.

The origins of the postcard view and the comic postcard may be found in the pictorial stationery that became popular during the 1840s. It was marketed by printers in seaside resorts and inland spas for holidaymakers and tourists. A local view, usually engraved or lithographed in black or brown, occupied the upper half of each sheet of notepaper, leaving space below for the message. Sometimes the illustration was a humorous sketch, perhaps depicting adventurous bathers, hapless oarsmen or disconsolate anglers, all subjects that later exercised the skills of comic postcard artists. Because it was essentially ephemeral and did not interest the early stamp collectors, pictorial stationery of this kind is now scarce.

In the 1850s another development in printing also acted as a forerunner to two familiar types of picture postcard, the photographic view and the portrait photograph. In 1854 a Paris photographer, André Disderi, adapted his cameras and plate-holders to take eight small negatives on each plate. The resultant photographs, measuring 4 by $2^1/2$ inches (100 by 65 mm), were known as cartes-de-visite because people exchanged them with friends. Personal photographs of this kind were soon supplemented by carte-de-visite portraits of such celebrities as members of the royal family, politicians, sportsmen and church dignitaries.

From these it was a small step to cartes-de-visite featuring comic characters, street vendors and musicians, labourers and beggars. Next came reproductions of well-known works of art and sets of posed episodes purporting to tell an amusing or a sentimental story. Such cartes-de-visite were usually sold at twopence or threepence each or in sets of six for a shilling. For almost fifty years cartes-de-visite remained the most popular kind of photograph, selling in huge numbers. They

9

Far left: *Gladys Cooper (1888-1971), the personification of the girl on the chocolate box, made her debut in 1905 in 'Bluebell in Fairyland'. She became a Gaiety Girl before ending her career gracefully in more serious roles in the cinema as well as the theatre. (Dover Street Studio)*

Left: *David Lloyd George, President of the Board of Trade in the Liberal government of 1905, later became Chancellor of the Exchequer and Prime Minister. (Philco)*

fell out of favour with the invention of roll film and Kodak cameras during the 1890s and were soon replaced by photographic postcards selling at a penny each.

Among the most popular of these were portraits of people in the public eye. The progressive widening of the parliamentary franchise during the nineteenth century stimulated a much keener interest in politics and politicians. Because newspaper pictures were of such poor quality and the more expensive periodicals preferred to feature royal personages, society beauties and stage and sporting celebrities, most ordinary voters had only the blurred portraits on cheaply printed election leaflets by which to recognise the politicians for whom they were invited to vote. During the 1890s postcard publishers began to fill this gap in the political spectrum. William Gladstone, who died in 1898, lived long enough to be portrayed on postcards, and the third Marquis of Salisbury, prime minister for the third time from 1895 until his retirement in 1902, was also portrayed in sombre and statesmanlike mood. Members of the Liberal government that took office after its landslide victory in the 1906 general election appear to have taken their politics a little less seriously. Sir Henry Campbell-Bannerman, prime minister until 1908, his successor, H. H. Asquith, and the irrepressible David Lloyd George were among the Liberal members who were happy to smile for the camera. Liberals and Conservatives were not the only politicians to be seen on postcards of the Edwardian period. Also on sale was 'The Star Album of 48 Post Cards, perforated for detaching, depicting in a lifelike manner our Pioneers of British Labour,

John Martin Harvey (1863-1944) became famous as Sydney Carton, the tragic hero of 'The Only Way', a dramatisation of Charles Dickens's novel 'A Tale of Two Cities'. First produced in 1899 at the Lyceum Theatre, off the Strand, 'The Only Way' was widely acclaimed by provincial audiences when taken on tour. (Rotary Photo)

Left: *Jack Hobbs (left) and Herbert Sutcliffe (right) open the innings for the Players against the Gentlemen at the Scarborough Cricket Festival in September 1931. (Iris Publishing)*

Above: Bradford-born Gertie Millar (1879-1952) was one of the stars of the musical comedies staged at the Gaiety Theatre, Aldwych, London, before the First World War. She later became Countess of Dudley. (Rotary Photo)

faithfully reproduced from original photographs, all being Members of the 1906 Parliament, with a short biography of each'.

Even more popular than the picture postcards of politicians were those that portrayed the stars of the Edwardian stage. As yet without the rivalry of radio, television or even the flickering silent films, the theatre offered entertainment for all tastes from the boisterous turns of the music-halls to the melodious and light-hearted musical comedies and the thought-provoking plays of the legitimate theatre. Picture postcards by the million paid tribute to the actors and actresses, comedians and musicians who provided this entertainment.

One of the most popular actresses was Gladys Cooper, whose postcard portraits invariably showed her in decorous poses, always sedately genteel and fashionably but never flamboyantly dressed. Her postcards enjoyed a longer run than those of most Edwardian actresses, for they were still being produced more than thirty years after her debut on her seventeenth birthday in 1905 at the Theatre Royal, Colchester, in *Bluebell in Fairyland*. Among the other theatrical beauties whose postcards could be bought during the Edwardian period for a penny each were Camille Clifford, Gertie Millar, Gabrielle Ray and the Dare sisters, Zena and Phyllis. Because lavish productions of historical dramas were so successful, many of the actors posed in costume for their postcards. John Martin Harvey in *The Only Way*, Fred Terry in *The Scarlet Pimpernel*, Lewis Waller in *Monsieur Beaucaire* and Henry Lytton in the comic operas of Gilbert and Sullivan were among the favourites of Edwardian theatre-goers. Every sizable town had at least one theatre among its amenities, and the touring companies used picture postcards to advertise their itineraries and their programmes as well as to provide attractive souvenirs for their patrons. To these portraits of professional actors and actresses may be added those of the many amateur performers who presented plays and musical comedies at local theatres, usually to raise funds for charity. A visit to the photographer's studio was part of the excitement of being able for one week at least to tread the boards in professional style.

A hand-cart, two horse-drawn carts and a girl on a bicycle show that Greengate, Stafford, was a busy thoroughfare in 1908, when this postcard was dated.

Topographicals

This view of 'Old Houses in Friar Street, Worcester, 1567' was painted for Raphael Tuck's Oilette series by Charles E. Flower (1871-1951).

Most people associate picture postcards with views of beaches, piers and promenades at seaside resorts or of mountains, lakes and forests in tourist centres. For postcards of this kind, for urban street scenes and general views, collectors use the term 'topographicals'. The early topographicals were in a standard form. Because one side of the postcard had to bear the postage stamp and the addressee's name and address, the other side had to accommodate both the picture and the message. The designer usually arranged three or four small vignettes across the top and down the left-hand edge of the card. The lower part was left blank for the message. The vignettes might show local beauty spots, historic buildings, monuments or memorials, the casino, the pump-room or even the railway station. Garlands of flowers or rustic work linked the vignettes, and the resort or spa was identified in an expression such as *Greetings from Niagara Falls, Souvenir de Biarritz, Saluti di Napoli* or *Gruss aus Marienbad*. As most of these early topographicals were sent by holidaymakers from Austria, Germany or German-speaking Switzerland, the German greeting was the most familiar, and collectors now refer to postcards in this design as '*Gruss aus* cards', regardless of where they originated. Between about 1880 and 1900 they were

The Glynne Arms public house at Himley, Staffordshire, is better known to Midlanders as the Crooked House because subsidence due to coal-mining has caused the building to tilt alarmingly. (John Steen & Co)

A little girl in white peeps over her shoulder at the camera on the Esplanade at Lowestoft in about 1905.

The Gordon tartan provides a frame for this view of Inverness Castle from the riverside walk. (Valentine & Sons)

by far the commonest type of postcard. Today examples in clean, undamaged condition, complete with the postage stamp and a neat, clear postmark, are likely to be difficult to find, especially if posted before about 1900 from countries that were then less accessible to tourists, such as Russia, Egypt and Palestine. In Britain, where postal

An Italian version of the 'Gruss aus' postcards, 'Un Saluto da Venezia', posted in 1903.

regulations hindered the introduction of topographicals until the 1890s, the preference was for cards with a single view, usually occupying most of the space available and leaving room only for the briefest of messages.

The limitations of early twentieth-century cameras, with their tripods, black hoods, cumbersome plates and slow shutter speeds, made taking topographical views of busy streets a difficult task for the photographer. His best plan was to set up his camera early on a sunny morning before the street was thronging with passers-by, many of whom would have ample leisure to stand and stare. Unfortunately the views produced at such a time tended to lack vitality. Collectors today are willing to pay a considerable premium for street scenes in which the photographer has captured plenty of movement, bustling pedestrians, horse-drawn vehicles and especially a close-up shot of a tram, a post office van or a costermonger's barrow. It is an interesting exercise to match modern views with those of the same places on postcards published many years ago.

Among the most prolific publishers of topographical postcards before

There are plenty of shoppers but no cars or buses in Corporation Street, Birmingham, on a sunny day about 1902. (H. P. Pope)

14

Above: *Light traffic in Lichfield Street, Wolverhampton, about 1910. The ornate building on the left is the Art Gallery. (Milton)*

Right: *Only horse-drawn traffic is to be seen in this view of London's Strand looking east, photographed by Louis Levy about 1905.*

The water cart fills up from the millpond at Mapledurham, near Pangbourne, Berkshire. (Frith & Co)

Motor cars and horse-drawn carriages keep to the right along the Avenue du Bois de Boulogne in this pre-1914 view of Paris with the Arc de Triomphe in the distance.

Above: *Peterborough Cathedral, one of a series of views printed by Raphael Tuck & Sons for the Great Eastern Railway Company.*

Right: *Window shopping in Birmingham was a popular pastime for Edwardian Midlanders, especially when the Midland Arcade offered shelter from the weather and relief from the bustling city streets.*

Straw boaters are popular among the strollers on Bournemouth Pier in this view taken by Louis Levy about 1907.

An open-decked tram is the only mechanised vehicle to be seen in St Patrick's Street, Cork, on this view, taken about 1905. The card was one of many given away free in such periodicals as 'Smart Novels', 'Dainty Novels' and 'The Weekly Tale-Teller'. (Shurey)

St. Patrick's Street, Cork.

783   PARIS. — Le Boulevard de la Madeleine.   L.L.

A Louis Levy view of heavy traffic in the Boulevard de la Madeleine, Paris, about 1910.

the First World War was a French photographer, Louis Levy, who also had a studio in London. Many of his street scenes are full of movement, but in Britain he confined his attention mainly to London, southern seaside resorts and tourist towns like Canterbury, Norwich and Stratford-upon-Avon. Levy's postcards can usually be identified by his initials in the caption. Other prominent British publishers of photographic views included Valentine & Sons of Dundee, E. Wrench Ltd of London, Millar & Lang of Glasgow and an Edinburgh pioneer, George Stewart, who produced a set of views of the Scottish capital as early as 1894. As well as publishing photographic views, many firms employed artists to produce topographical postcards. Among those whose work is particularly popular with collectors are Alfred R. Quinton (1853-1934), who worked mainly for J. Salmon Ltd of Sevenoaks, Charles E. Flower (1871-1951), who provided views for Raphael Tuck's Oilette series, introduced in 1903, and Walter H. Young (1870-1920), who worked for several publishers, signing his sketches with the pseudonym Jotter.

Comic cards

Although by the 1890s most magazines and popular newspapers were illustrated with photographs as well as line drawings, artists in black and white still dominated the humorous periodicals and children's literature of all kinds. It was easy for talented artists to make the transition to comic postcards, which offered greater scope for those who also liked to work in colour. Among the many artists who drew comic postcards as well as illustrations for books and magazines were Tom Browne, René Bull, John Hassall, Phil May, Will Owen and W. Heath Robinson, each with his own distinctive style. The most prolific British comic artist was Donald McGill (1875-1962), whose postcards sold in millions at seaside resorts. His cartoons of plump bathers, cheeky children, buxom girls and hen-pecked husbands were often badly drawn and garishly coloured but they formed a recognisable genre whose popularity attracted many imitators. Another artist whose work is instantly identifiable was Louis Wain (1860-1939), best known

Several firms have published postcards featuring silhouettes. This example, of First World War vintage, is from a series entitled 'Camp Life'. (Photochrom Co)

ALL MY OWN WORK BY GRIMES — With acknowledgments To "THE STAR"

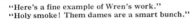

"Here's a fine example of Wren's work."
"Holy smoke! Them dames are a smart bunch."

WHEN FATHER LAID THE CARPET.

Above: *Born in Nottingham, Tom Browne (1872-1910) moved to London as a young man and produced postcards for several publishers, as well as contributing to a wide range of periodicals. His early death prevented his developing into a serious artist. (Davidson Bros)*

Left: *A Second World War cartoon by Grimes for the 'Star' features an American serviceman who apparently confuses Sir Christopher Wren with the Women's Royal Naval Service. (Raphael Tuck & Sons)*

Right: *Diabolo, the spinning top game, caricatured by Tom Browne on this 1908 postcard. (Davidson Bros)*

Left: *Many of Tom Browne's postcard sketches were in the style of the comic papers such as 'Chips' and 'Comic Cuts'. 'Blow your whistle, that's a foul!' says the captain. 'Can't, I've swallowed it!' is the hapless referee's reply. (Davidson Bros)*

19

for his amusing drawings of cats lightly disguised as human beings. An album of 320 Louis Wain postcards was sold at Phillips's auction rooms for £2200 as long ago as 1986.

Comic postcards naturally reflect the social environment of their time. Favourite pastimes in the early years of the twentieth century, such as ping-pong, roller-skating, billiards and diabolo, provided postcard artists with ample material, as did newfangled gadgets like the telephone, the motor car and the aeroplane, all of them difficult to take seriously at that early stage of their development. Every aspect of contemporary life was covered by the comic artists, so that it was possible to buy postcards poking fun at politicians and their policies, at foreign potentates and their pretensions and even at the militant suffragettes seeking votes for women. The two world wars brought new topics for comic postcards, among them food rationing, the black-out, raw recruits, irascible sergeant-majors and Land Army girls. Bruce Bairnsfather (1888-1959), creator of Old Bill, the sardonic, walrus-moustached veteran warrior typifying the British Tommy, was a notable chronicler of the humours of army life during the First World War.

This cat in khaki, sketched by Louis Wain (1860-1939), known as 'the man who drew cats', appears on a Raphael Tuck postcard of 1915.

In lighter vein were the postcards designed over a long period by Mabel Lucie Attwell (1879-1964). She specialised in chubby children, captioning their antics with catchphrases or sentimental verse. The American artist Charles Dana Gibson (1867-1944) catered for more adult tastes. His creation, the tall and graceful young woman with the bouffant hairstyle, the trim waist and flowing skirts, became known as the Gibson Girl. She was featured in decorous sketches in series of postcards illustrating such fashionable themes as golfing, motoring and courting. In 1904 she was personified on the London stage by

Donald McGill (1875-1962) is best remembered for his comic seaside postcards featuring such perennial favourites as plump bathers, red-nosed inebriates, cheeky children and large landladies. This example of his work, posted in 1912, is more genteel. (Joseph Asher & Co)

Above left: *'In harbour' is sufficient caption for this Danish postcard – the picture tells all. (K. Witt-Moller)*

Above right: *Introduced as a volunteer force in 1907, the Territorial Army, popularly known as the Terriers, was the butt of much good-natured humour but proved its worth when war came in 1914. This valiant warrior was drawn by Frederick Gothard (1882-1971), who used the pseudonym Spatz. (Thomas Hind)*

Left: *This chubby child is instantly recognisable as a creation of Mabel Lucie Attwell (1879-1964). (Valentine & Sons)*

21

By changing the name in the caption, comic cards of this type could be sold at other seaside resorts. (Valentine & Sons)

I HAVE JUST ARRIVED AT EASTBOURNE

Roller-skating had its hazards, as shown in this postcard sketch by Harry Payne (1888-1940). (A. & G. Taylor)

Camille Clifford, who, in *The Catch of the Season* at the Vaudeville Theatre, sang 'Why do they call me a Gibson Girl?'.

In comparison with the cartoons on comic postcards published before about 1920, those on more modern postcards are less competently drawn, more aggressively coloured and certainly more Rabelaisian in their wit. A collection spanning the twentieth century vividly reflects changing tastes in art and humour.

Although specialising in military subjects, the Aldershot firm of Gale & Polden also published humorous postcards such as this example from a series entitled 'Before Our Time'.

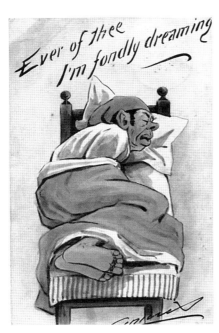

Left: *A Christmas postcard by George F. Christie, a Scottish artist who produced comic cards for several publishers. (W. Ritchie & Sons)*

Above left: *Martin Anderson (1854-1932), a Scottish artist whose pseudonym was Cynicus, formed his own company in Tayport, Fife, to publish his comic postcards. (Cynicus Publishing Co)*

Below left: *'Any Port in a Storm', a Tuck's Oilette drawn by James A. Duncan, who signed his postcard sketches as Hamish.*

Left: *This sketch by Comicus, the pseudonym of Harry Parlett, has a space in the caption for the sender to add the name of the resort to which he is sticking!*

Commemoratives

At a time when television had still to be invented and newspaper photographs were generally of poor quality, the clearest and most vivid pictures of an event such as a fire, a flood, a railway accident or a royal visit were often provided in the form of postcards produced by local photographers. On 3rd October 1904 an express train, travelling at speed as it approached Loughor bridge near Llanelli in south Wales, left the rails and crashed down the embankment. Two photographers, one from Swansea and the other from London, were quickly on the scene. The picture postcards made from their photographs were on sale a few days later at a penny each. Today collectors expect to pay high prices for postcards of this and other serious railway accidents dating from before about 1920. Because motor vehicles and aeroplanes were comparatively recent innovations, any mishap resulting in loss of life was also of sufficient public interest to justify the production of picture postcards.

In many countries during the early years of the twentieth century there was a succession of exhibitions, trade fairs, pageants and agricultural shows. Picture postcards faithfully recorded their manifold attractions. At the larger exhibitions there was usually a temporary post office where a commemorative postmark was applied to the mail, an added inducement to visitors to buy and post souvenir postcards.

A typical 'Hands across the Sea' greetings card posted in 1908. (Wildt & Kray)

STILL SENDING KINDLY GREETING,
AND IN REMEMBRANCE MEETING · ⋮ ·

The Edwardian period was the heyday of the large exhibitions at the site known as the Great White City at Shepherd's Bush in west London. The Franco-British Exhibition in 1908 (left), the Imperial International Exhibition in 1909 and the Japanese-British Exhibition in 1910 (below left) were all publicised by special picture postcards, most of them views but others gently humorous. The giant Flip-flap (below right) was a popular attraction for visitors with a head for heights.

Below: Launched at John Brown's Clyde shipyard in 1923, the 'Franconia' sailed on the Cunard North American service. After being used as a troopship during the Second World War she returned to her peacetime service in 1949.

Smash of the "FLYING WELSHMAN," October 3rd, 1904. —*Copyright.*

When the 'Flying Welshman' crashed at Loughor bridge on 3rd October 1904, a Swansea photographer, Jack Lewis, was quickly on the spot to record the scene on picture postcards.

Eight million people visited the Franco-British Exhibition at Shepherd's Bush, London, in 1908, and, judging by the number of postcards that have survived, many visitors must have patronised the postcard kiosks. Other large exhibitions commemorated by picture postcards included the Paris Exposition in 1900, the St Louis World's Fair in 1904, the Japanese-British Exhibition at Shepherd's Bush in 1910 and the Wembley exhibitions of 1924 and 1925. Much more difficult to find are the postcards emanating from small local exhibitions such as those held at Cork and Wolverhampton in 1902 and at Nottingham in 1903.

One of the first royal occasions for which picture postcards were published in Britain was the Diamond Jubilee of Queen Victoria in 1897. Examples of these are now scarce, but postcards marking her death four years later are still fairly easy to acquire. The British and other European royal families seldom appeared in anything but the most formal of photographs, many of them carefully posed in a court photographer's studio. The staid sepia or black and white portraits of Edward VII and his children contrast sharply with the colour postcards of the present royal family.

George Stewart & Company of Edinburgh, pioneers of topographical postcards in Britain, also published some of the first postcards to commemorate a military campaign, the Sudanese expedition commanded by Sir Herbert Kitchener that culminated in his victory over the dervishes at Omdurman in 1898. One design featured Kitchener's portrait with vignettes of Khartoum, a charging lancer and a bust of General Gordon decked with flags and a laurel wreath. The outbreak of the Boer War in 1899 brought topical postcards from Stewart, from other publishers in Britain and from several European countries that favoured the Boer cause. The Boxer Rebellion in China, the Russo-Japanese War and the war between Italy and Turkey in 1911-12 were all marked by picture postcards, some photographic and others with propaganda cartoons.

The Great Western Railway's Fishguard Boat Express bound for the Irish steamer in Raphael Tuck's series of 'Famous Expresses', 1908.

Measuring 750 feet (229 metres) in length and with a displacement of 42,500 tons (43,180 tonnes), the 'Empress of Britain' was launched in 1931 at John Brown's Clyde shipyard for the Canadian Pacific North American service. Requisitioned in 1939 for transporting troops, the ship was torpedoed by a German U-boat off the Irish coast in October 1940. (C.R. Hoffmann)

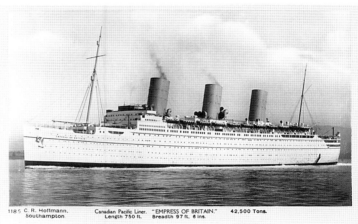

The First World War brought an avalanche of postcards of all kinds, topographical, humorous, sentimental and commemorative. The *Daily Mail* published more than twenty sets of postcards, each set reproducing eight different photographs of war scenes taken by official photographers. The two types of postcard particularly popular with soldiers on the Western Front were sketches of daintily under-dressed young ladies by such artists as Raphael Kirchner, Suzanne Meunier and Xavier Sager, and, to send home to wives and sweethearts, silk embroidered cards. Some of these bore sentimental messages or patriotic slogans embellished with sprays of flowers and foliage. Others featured regimental badges or national flags and coats of arms. Despite their tawdry quality, primitive colouring and cliché-ridden inscriptions, these embroidered postcards remain among the most evocative souvenirs of that grim conflict.

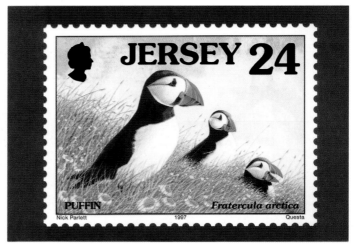

This Jersey postcard reproduces the 24p stamp in the 1997 series featuring wild birds. The stamps and postcards were designed by Nick Parlett and printed by the House of Questa.

Philately

Many early plain and picture postcards fell victim to the scissors of stamp collectors. Most stamp albums provided a small ruled space for each stamp, including those only printed on plain postcards. Corners were snipped from these, and also from picture postcards so that the adhesive stamps could be soaked off and mounted in the allotted spaces. When loose-leaf albums became popular during the 1930s stamp collectors generally lost interest in postcards, often preferring stamps in mint condition, unsullied by a postmark. Some thirty years passed before postcards again came to be regarded as acceptable for a philatelic collection and modern stamp collectors keep their postcards intact. To snip off a corner would now be considered an act of vandalism.

Postcards whose designs reproduce new commemorative stamps are obviously aimed at stamp collectors. The British Post Office introduced postcards of this kind in 1973 when the 3p stamp in a series honouring the cricketer W. G. Grace was also issued as a picture postcard. Since then several hundred different British commemorative stamps have been reproduced as postcards. Other countries where similar postcards are issued regularly include Austria, Liechtenstein, Portugal and the Isle of Man. A postcard reproducing a postage stamp becomes a 'maximum' card when an example of the stamp it features is affixed to the picture side and postmarked. For a '100 per cent maximum' the postmark should also have a design closely associated with the subject of the postcard and stamp. The early postage stamps, with their portraits of reigning monarchs or presidents, coats of arms or figures of value, offered little scope for the production of maximum cards. As the range

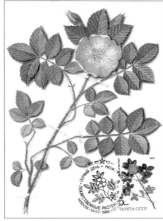

Far left: *Raphael Santi's 'Portrait of a Youth', in the Museum of Fine Arts, Budapest, on a Hungarian maximum card issued in 1968.*

Left: *A Russian maximum card with a dog rose depicted on the postcard, the 5 kopeck stamp issued in 1985, and the postmark.*

11p
Winnie-the-Pooh
The Year of the Child

ROWLAND HILL 1795-1879

Far left: *To publicise 1979 as the International Year of the Child the British Post Office issued stamps and postcards recalling favourite children's stories. The 11p stamp, on this postcard, was designed by Edward Hughes and based on E. H. Shepard's familiar illustrations. (Harrison & Sons)*

Left: *The British 10p stamp shown on this postcard was one of a series designed by Eric Stemp and issued in 1979 to mark the centenary of the death of Sir Rowland Hill. (Harrison & Sons)*

of subjects for stamp designs widened, particularly during the 1930s, maximum cards became more attractive and much easier to obtain. They first became popular in France, where there was a plentiful choice of both pictorial stamps and matching picture postcards for collectors to use as maximum cards. In Britain the Post Office was less accommodating, regarding postcards with the stamp on the picture side as a hindrance to the speedy handling of the mail. With the introduction in 1973 of the British postcards reproducing the designs of current commemorative stamps the production of maximum cards became easier, but the Post Office continued to regard such cards as 'embarrassing' and to advise that a stamped envelope should be enclosed with any request for maximum cards to be postmarked, so that these could be returned under cover. A picture postcard having the stamp on the picture side and posted in the normal way is likely to arrive at its destination with the postmark in its customary position on the address side and the stamp cancelled by the postman's biro. Despite this hazard,

Far left: *This red squirrel comes from a 1977 series depicting British wild animals in designs by Patrick Oxenham. (Harrison & Sons)*

Left: *North Sea oil is among the energy resources featured in a 1978 series of British stamps designed by Peter Murdoch and reproduced on postcards. (Harrison & Sons)*

maximum cards continue to be widely collected and early examples are now expensive. Equally popular with stamp collectors are postcards issued as part of a series of adhesive stamps. Between 1910 and 1937 the Swiss Post Office made an annual issue of picture postcards to publicise the National Festival. Since 1938 stamps have been issued instead of postcards, but collectors regard the latter as an integral part of the series and are willing to pay a good deal for some of the scarcer issues.

Particularly interesting to students of postal history and the carriage of mail are postcards whose postmarks indicate the route or the means of transport by which they have travelled. In the days when liners carried passengers and mail across the oceans of the world, shipping companies used picture postcards to publicise their ships and services. By international agreement passengers posting mail on board a ship were allowed to frank it with the ordinary postage stamps of the country to which the ship belonged. If the mail was then landed in a

A Swiss post coach pauses on a mountain road near St Moritz in 1910. (Photoglob Co)

The Isle of Man Post Office has issued several series of postcards reproducing stamps that portray winners of the TT motorcycle races. Among them is Jimmie Simpson, winner of the 1932 Senior TT race. This 1982 issue was designed by J. H. Nicholson and printed by the House of Questa.

1932 SENIOR TT RACE

E II R

JIMMIE SIMPSON
1922 - 1934

TT RACE WINNER
& FIRST RIDER
TO LAP AT
60, 70 & 80 MPH

24P

ISLE OF MAN

J.H. NICHOLSON RI   1982   QUESTA

foreign port for onward despatch, the local office used a special post-mark embodying the French word *paquebot* to explain why the stamps of a different country were accepted as valid for postage. It is possible to form an attractive collection of picture postcards featuring liners and with British postage stamps postmarked in foreign ports all over the world. Between 1905 and 1914 ships of the White Star Line and the American Line sailing between British ports and New York carried their own post offices staffed by British and American clerks. These offices used distinctive postmarks reading 'Transatlantic Post Office'. Other postmarks, among them 'Sea Post Office', 'Posted on Board' and 'Postad Ombord', have been used on mail posted at sea in other parts of the world. Picture postcards dating from before 1939 and featuring cross-Channel steamers may be found with postmarks including the letters MB or BM. These are the initials of the words 'mobile box' or the French equivalent, *boîte mobile*, indicating that the postcards were posted in special letter boxes placed on the quayside and taken on board when the ship sailed.

Like the shipping lines, railway companies have often used picture postcards to advertise their services. Before the British railway system was taken into public ownership in 1948 several of the companies issued series of post-cards with views of seaside resorts and inland towns served by their lines. Other series repro-duced in miniature the colourful posters to be seen on every railway station. Even more popu-lar with railway enthusiasts are the postcards of locomotives, many dating from the days of steam. Interest and philatelic value are added

Below: *This postcard reproduces the 12p stamp in a series issued in Guernsey in 1981 to celebrate the wedding of the Prince of Wales and Lady Diana Spencer. (Guernsey Post Office)*

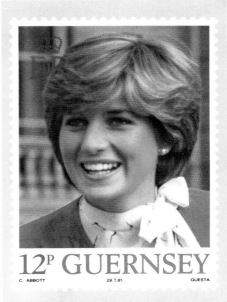

12P GUERNSEY

C. ABBOTT   29.7.81   QUESTA

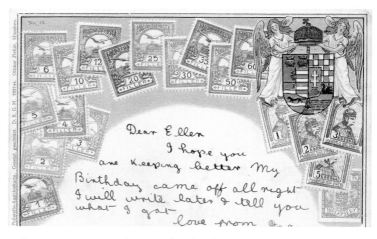

Before the First World War several publishers produced postcards on which the space for the message was framed by an assortment of postage stamps. This example, showing the 1900 series of Hungarian stamps, was published by Ottmar Zieher, of Munich, who usually added a coat of arms to the design.

to such postcards when they bear postmarks showing that they have been posted or sorted on one of the railway travelling post offices or sorting carriages. The initials TPO (travelling post office), SC (sorting carriage) or ST (sorting tender) usually indicate the railway association, and most postmarks of this kind also include the names of the termini served by the train. In other countries, among them Australia, Ireland and the United States, the initials RPO (railway post office) are normally used, and in France the railway postmarks have a distinctive scalloped frame. *Ambulante* and *ambulancia* are the words to look for in Belgian and Portuguese railway post-marks, *Bahnpost* for German, Austrian and Swiss railways. As the neat, clear postmark of a *paquebot* or a travelling post office may more than double the value of a postcard, the collector is wise to check every postmark carefully.

Finally mention must be made of the attractive picture postcards now being issued by many national postal museums. Their subjects range over every aspect of the postal services, from the uniforms of post office employees to the vehicles that have been used at different periods for the transport of mail, and from reproductions of rare stamps to portraits of postal pioneers and celebrities. Notable series of museum postcards have come from Copenhagen, Oslo and Stockholm.

A Rio de Janeiro postman of 1849 delivers a letter on this Brazilian Postal Museum postcard in a series featuring post office uniforms. (Ivan Rodrigues)

The 'Daily Mail' war postcards published in twenty-two series, each of eight cards, were inscribed as 'Passed by Censor'. This example shows a British heavy gun in action.

Collecting

Collecting picture postcards can justifiably be regarded as the first of the indoor collecting hobbies to enjoy universal popularity. Before the opening years of the twentieth century coins, medallions, prints and autographs had all been collected by small and wealthy coteries, mostly male, while postage stamps had attracted schoolboys and elderly gentlemen. But picture postcards appealed to both sexes and to all age groups and social classes, for many of whom collecting was a new phenomenon. Part of the reason lay in the cheapness and easy availability of picture postcards. At a cost of no more than a halfpenny or a penny each they could be bought from any bookseller, stationer, newsagent or tobacconist, at railway station kiosks, in hotel lobbies and at every village store. Many were given away free with family magazines and cheap novels or by railway and shipping companies. The pictures illustrated almost every conceivable theme and topic. People interested in wild flowers, military uniforms, foreign travel, heraldry, stage celebrities, royal personages, steam locomotives or seaside humour could all find postcards to their taste.

Before the First World War housing a postcard collection was equally inexpensive. An album accommodating

'Keeping a sharp look out' is the caption on this 'Daily Mail' postcard showing a First World War Tommy in a sandbagged observation post.

ninety-six cards could be bought for 6¹/₂d or 10 cents, while a pound or a few dollars would buy a large leather-bound album with spaces for several hundred cards. To encourage the hobby, some of the large publishers ran competitions for collectors. In 1900 Raphael Tuck & Sons offered prizes of up to £1000 for the largest collections of Tuck's postcards that had been sent through the post. The winning entry numbered over twenty thousand cards, and a second competition in 1902 was won by a collector who had amassed a total of more than twenty-five thousand cards. A magazine devoted to the hobby, *The Picture Postcard*, was launched in London in 1900, and the popular illustrated journals frequently published articles about postcards. In *The Quiver* in 1906 a reporter described his visits to three London companies, Raphael Tuck & Sons, the Rotary Photographic Company and J. Beagles & Company.

All this activity came to a halt with the outbreak of the First World War. The interruption of international communications, the restrictions of wartime censorship, rising production costs, the general preoccupation with more serious matters and finally, in June 1918, the increase in the postage on postcards in Britain from a halfpenny to a penny combined to end postcard collecting as an organised hobby. During the Second World War many albums of old picture postcards were put out as waste paper for salvage, and many others must have been destroyed in air raids.

The Prince of Wales, later King Edward VIII, wears the uniform of the Welsh Guards in this Raphael Tuck postcard.

The revival of the hobby during the early 1970s has been variously attributed to stamp collectors' dissatisfaction with the relentless flood of expensive new issues of stamps from so many countries, to the stimulus given to the visual arts by expanding television services and to nostalgia for the vanished world of the early twentieth century. Many collectors choose serious historical and social themes, among them the development of aviation, the campaign for women's suffrage, polar exploration, political cartoons and the cinema of the 1930s. Equally attractive collections can also be formed on less ambitious themes such as sundials, Union Castle liners, parrots, angling and pierrot troupes. Although most collectors limit their interest to postcards published before a particular date, perhaps 1914, 1920 or 1950, there is a growing demand for modern cards reflecting contemporary events. Pop musicians, football and cricket stars, the royal family, television personalities and prime ministers past, present or potential all have their devotees, and dozens of publishers are now producing postcards

on these and similar topics. Because some print runs are comparatively small, postcards of this type tend to be more expensive than the normal views and comic postcards.

A theme popular before the First World War was revived in the 1990s with the issue of long series of postcards showing military uniforms in full colour. One publisher, the Pompadour Gallery, offered more than thirty sets, each containing six postcards. As well as familiar British regiments, these featured the French Foreign Legion, the United States Marine Corps and the regiments of Canada. Another publisher, Geoff White, provided a wide range of military postcards in sets of six, with the Royal Marines, the Yeomanry Cavalry, the Brigade of Gurkhas and the Scottish regiments on parade.

The hobby of postcard collecting has no prestigious central body such as the Royal Philatelic Society or the Royal Numismatic Society but most large towns in Britain and many in the United States have a local society run on informal lines, with regular meetings at which members can display their treasures and exchange or auction their spare cards. The more enterprising societies stage exhibitions at local museums or art galleries, some of which now also hold reference collections of postcards with local associations.

Collectors are also sustained by a wide range of dealers, large and small. A typical issue of *Picture Postcard Monthly* (see Further reading)

Above left:
Ellaline Terriss (1871-1971), for a time one of the Gaiety Girls, married Seymour Hicks in 1902 and with him managed the Vaudeville Theatre in the Strand, London. (J. Beagles)

Above right:
Postcard reproductions of well-known posters have added value if autographed by the artist, such as this example by W. H. Caffyn.

Above left: *This irresistible sailor was among the merry matelots in the Celesque series published by the Photochrom Company during the First World War.*

Above right: *Field Marshals Paul von Hindenburg (1847-1934) and Erich von Ludendorff (1865-1938), German commanders in the First World War.*

Above left: *Overprinted for use as a Christmas card, this Oilette postcard shows a patrol of 21st Lancers passing Marlborough House, London. (Raphael Tuck & Sons)*

Above right: *Informative text on the back is a feature of military postcards published by the Pompadour Gallery, Romford. This example, by Bryan Fosten, shows a private of the Black Watch, the Royal Highland Regiment, in France in 1917.*

Above left: *An American War Savings postcard issued in 1943 by the US Treasury Department.*

Above right: *The poster reproduced on this postcard advertised the greetings telegram service introduced by the GPO in 1935. (British Telecom)*

Above left: *Sweet dreams for the soldier on this modern Italian card published by Edizioni Saemer.*

Above right: *Between 1905 and its demise in 1939 the firm of Misch & Company published high-quality reproductions of well-known works of art. Most were printed in Germany, such as 'La Belle Ferronnière', a Leonardo da Vinci portrait in the Louvre collection in Paris.*

contains display advertisements for dealers and auctioneers offering postcards among other collectables, and for local stamp, coin and post-card fairs. With the help of the reference department of the local public library the newcomer to postcard collecting should have no difficulty in making contact with other enthusiasts or in discovering the litera-ture devoted to the hobby.

As with other collectables, the value of old picture postcards is deter-mined mainly by supply and demand. The revival of the hobby during the early 1970s prompted a few large stamp-dealing firms to add post-cards to their wares. The demand from firms anxious to build up adequate stocks forced up the prices of many popular types of post-card. As an example, the comic cards designed between 1900 and 1910 by the Nottingham artist Tom Browne could be bought at 6d ($2^1/2$p) each in 1970. Within a few years they were costing £1.50 each, although prices have not continued to rise so steeply. Many similar instances could be quoted. Auction realisations, often mentioned in the press when they seem abnormally high, are an unreliable basis for valuation since competition between two determined bidders with ample means can raise prices to extraordinary levels. Postcard fairs offer a better chance of bargains, while the sales lists or approval selections of reli-able dealers enable the collector to make purchases at leisure and after due consideration. It is prudent to reject, even at bargain prices, post-cards that have been damaged or soiled. Faults to look for include scuffed or rounded corners, foxing (the brown stains caused by storage in damp conditions), fading on photographic cards and traces of the stamp hav-ing been removed, usually by steaming, from the corner of a card.

Storing postcards in a damp cupboard can cause even worse damage than foxing. Old picture postcards were made like sandwiches, with a piece of thin cardboard between two layers of good quality paper on which the picture and the inscriptions were printed. Dampness de-stroys the adhesive that binds the three elements together so that they gradually become detached and the postcard disintegrates. A hazard of using the old-fashioned corner-slot albums was that the corners of the postcards could easily be bent or broken while being inserted in the album. To read the message or to examine the stamp and postmark, it was necessary to remove the postcard from the album, adding to the possibility of damage. The modern album leaves with transparent pock-ets into which the postcards can be slipped enable both sides of the cards to be seen simply by turning the page. As these albums are also loose-leaf, rearranging the collection is an easy matter. The chemical softener used in the manufacture of some of these transparent pockets is reported to have damaged old photographic cards but a refined form of polypropylene known as polyprotec is claimed to be completely safe for housing all kinds of postcards. There is a wide range of such albums on the market, most of them with either four or six pockets to the page. Dealers who file their stock in cardboard boxes normally put each postcard in an envelope made with a clear polypropylene front and a plain white paper back. These envelopes are dust- and moisture-proof and can be bought quite cheaply in several sizes to accommodate different types of postcard.

Glossary

Bookmark: a postcard in the shape of a bookmark, measuring about $1^3/_4$ by $5^1/_2$ inches (45 by 140 mm). Most pre-1914 types featured portraits of royalty or theatrical celebrities.

Court size: a slightly squarer type of postcard measuring $3^1/_2$ by $4^1/_2$ inches (89 by 115 mm), introduced in 1895 and used for many undivided-back postcards. Superseded in 1899 by the standard-size card, $3^1/_2$ by $5^1/_2$ inches (89 by 140 mm).

Deltiology: the American term for postcard collecting.

Divided back: a postcard on which one side was divided, usually by a vertical line, to accommodate both the message and the addressee's name and address. Introduced in Britain in 1902 and adopted in other countries within a few years.

Fantasy: generally accepted to mean the montage postcard on which the portrait of a celebrity is composed of the ingeniously contorted bodies of young women. Another type features dozens of babies' faces gazing from incongruous places such as birds' nests in a tree, rows of cabbages in a garden or a basket of apples.

Glitter: the brightly coloured powdered glass or mica used to decorate greetings postcards, views and the dresses of ladies in portrait photographs. Postal workers in many countries feared ill effects from the glitter or tinsel and refused to handle such postcards. In Britain after 1907 postcards of this type had to be enclosed in an envelope before posting.

Gruss aus: the early type of topographical postcard with vignette views on the message side and the caption *Gruss aus ...* or its equivalent in other languages to identify the place depicted.

Heraldic: postcards on which a coat of arms in full colour is the main or a prominent feature of the design. Stoddart & Company of Halifax published over a thousand such cards under the trade name 'Ja-Ja'. Another Halifax firm, S. Oates & Company, depicted the popular Goss souvenir china ornaments on which coats of arms formed the decoration.

Hold-to-light: when this type of postcard is held against a strong light extra details or colours are added to the design where transparent paper has been incorporated in the card.

Maximum: an innovation of the 1930s consisting of a picture postcard that has a postage stamp in the same or a closely related design affixed to the picture side and postmarked. For a 100 per cent maximum card the design of the postmark should also reflect the subject of the postcard and stamp. Many countries now issue picture postcards reproducing the designs of new commemorative stamps, so making maximum cards easy to produce.

Midget: several British publishers marketed square or diamond-shaped cards which were half the size of a normal postcard. Most of these midget cards featured portraits of stage celebrities or members of the royal family and were popular between about 1902 and 1910.

Oilette: the name given by Raphael Tuck & Sons to their wide range of picture postcards reproducing paintings in oils or watercolours, most of them specially commissioned from talented artists. Introduced in 1903, the series included topographical views, historical scenes, portraits, cartoons, regimental uniforms and many other subjects. Oilettes remained the most popular British picture postcards until the 1930s.

Postal card: the philatelic term for a plain postcard on which the postage stamp has been printed before issue.

Pull-out: a postcard with a small flap as part of the design, perhaps as a postman's bag, a shopping basket, a miniature envelope or a suitcase. The flap could be lifted to release a strip of tiny views folded concertina-wise below it.

Silk: three types of silk postcard were marketed by various firms before 1920. The coloured designs were woven in silk, embroidered or printed on silk before being affixed to the postcard backing.

Topographical: a view of an urban or a rural scene, more attractive to collectors if also showing horse-drawn or early motor vehicles.

Undivided back: a postcard on which one side accommodated the picture and the written message while the other was left blank for the addressee's name and address and the postage stamp.

Write-away: a type of comic postcard on which the cartoon is captioned by the first few words of a sentence left for the sender to complete. Examples are: 'I have no time ...' accompanying a sketch of an elderly gentleman being robbed of his watch by a fleet-footed thief; and 'I hope to see you ...' with a picture of a bewhiskered coastguard whose telescope is trained on girls bathing in the sea.

Further reading

Alderson, Frederick. *The Comic Postcard in English Life*. David & Charles, 1970.

Bray, Maurice I. *Railway Picture Postcards*. Moorland Publishing, 1986.

Byatt, Anthony. *Picture Postcards and Their Publishers*. Golden Age Postcard Books, 1978. Covers the period 1894-1939.

Carline, Richard. *Pictures in the Post*. Gordon Fraser, 1971.

Hill, C.W. *Edwardian Entertainments, A Picture Postcard View*. MAB Publishing, 1978.

Holt, Tonie and Valmai. *Picture Postcards of the Golden Age*. MacGibbon & Kee, 1971. Covers the period 1870-1918.

Monahan, Valerie. *Collecting Postcards in Colour, 1914-1930*. Blandford Press, 1980.

Monahan, Valerie. *An American Postcard Collector's Guide*. Blandford Press, 1981.

Staff, Frank. *The Picture Postcard and Its Origins*. Lutterworth Press, 1966.

Woolley, Eric. *The Black Country, A Portrait in Old Picture Postcards* (two volumes). SB Publications, 1988 and 1990.

MAGAZINE

Picture Postcard Monthly, 15 Debdale Lane, Keyworth, Nottingham NG12 5HT. Website: www. postcardcollecting.co.uk Monthly.

A London postman of 1820 is among the 'Postmen of the British Empire' in a series of fourteen given with Colman's starch.